Original title:
Nebulous Nonsense

Copyright © 2025 Creative Arts Management OÜ
All rights reserved.

Author: Lucas Harrington
ISBN HARDBACK: 978-1-80567-785-7
ISBN PAPERBACK: 978-1-80567-906-6

Dreams in a Distorted Mirror

Reflections twist like silly string,
A cat in boots starts to sing.
Pigs dance high on candy trains,
While teacups laugh at sunlight rains.

Marshmallow clouds float by with glee,
And jellybeans grow on the trees.
A toaster says, "Let's fly away!"
While socks debate the rules of play.

The Jester's Eloquent Riddle

A jester juggles purple pies,
As owls skateboard through the skies.
He whispers secrets to a broom,
While llamas dance in disco gloom.

The riddle wraps in silly beats,
As shoelaces tap their tiny feet.
"If fish could fly, what would they wear?"
The crowd erupts in wild despair.

Shadows of a Forgotten Fable

In shadows cast by tuba sounds,
A dragon sips on merry rounds.
He wears a hat made out of cheese,
While unicorns whistle in the breeze.

Once there was a tale so bright,
It danced away in moonlit night.
A parrot plays a game of chess,
Against a frog in Sunday dress.

A Symphony of Scatterbrained Thoughts

A symphony of twirls and spins,
Where cats are dressed as violinists.
The music flows like sticky glue,
As pickle boats sail right on cue.

Ducklings ride on roller coasters,
And time forgets its usual posters.
With giggles caught in paper nets,
The symphony plays what sound forgets.

Voices of Vexing Vapors

Bubbles speak in ancient tongues,
While wispy tales are spun by nuns.
A cloud of giggles sweeps the room,
As shadows dance and fortunes loom.

Whispers float on zephyr's breath,
Tickling ears, then fading dead.
A jester's grin in every mist,
With secrets wrapped in vapor's twist.

The Curious Case of Vanishing Violets

Violets sprout where once they stood,
In gardens spry, beneath the wood.
With every blink, they turn to tea,
As squirrels giggle with pure glee.

A juggling frog leaps through the air,
Chasing shades that vanish fair.
Petals scatter like confetti,
A flower's riddle, oh so petty!

Echoes of Enigmatic Elysium

In fields of thought where echoes reign,
Surreal tunes dance on the brain.
Mirthful ghosts in waltz they twirl,
Creating chaos in a whirl.

Laughter lingers, then takes flight,
As dawn breaks with a tease of night.
Chasing dreams with playful glee,
Atop the clouds, we're wild and free!

The Twilight Tangle

In twilight's glow, where shadows play,
Socks entwine in a funny way.
A cat wearing glasses, reading a book,
Mischief lurks with every look.

Giggling trees bend to the ground,
As whispers of nonsense spin around.
With every twist, the world sways,
In a maze of mirth, we jest and play.

Charm of the Chaotic Cosmos

Stars wear pajamas in endless night,
Planets play tag, oh what a sight!
Galaxies laugh in a spiral dance,
Comets in tutus, taking a chance.

Black holes giggle, pulling things in,
While moonbeams tap-dance on silver skin.
Asteroids juggling in space's vast show,
Wishing upon wishes as they twinkle and glow.

Echoes of Elusive Euphoria

A giggle floats from a distant star,
Jellybean moons, oh how bizarre!
Whispers of joy swirl in the throng,
Dancing with shadows while humming a song.

Laughing suns shine, tickling the day,
Clouds trade secrets in a comical way.
Time takes a tumble, stumbles and falls,
Winding in circles, ignoring the calls.

Circus of the Cosmic Clouds

Cotton candy comets, bright pink and spun,
Elephants floating, oh what fun!
Ringmaster Saturn waves with delight,
As stardust performers twirl through the night.

Marshmallow meteors bounce on the scene,
Funny-faced rockets, bright and serene.
Juggling light beams in loops and in spins,
Where laughter is lost but never quite ends.

Whirling Whispers of What Could Be

Whirling whispers float on a breeze,
What if the stars could just tease?
Thoughts in a tumble, ideas that play,
Chasing the moonbeams, bright as the day.

Clouds wear hats, dapper and neat,
While rainbows dance on ballet feet.
Tickles of laughter in the void so wide,
Where truth is a paradox, hiding inside.

Threads of Thought and Twisted Torment

In a world where cats wear hats,
And squirrels converse in rhymes,
The clocks tick backward, laughing loud,
While polka-dots throw fancy primes.

A tangle of socks begins to dance,
As jellybeans take to the skies,
With dapper ants in shiny pants,
Spinning tales of sweet surprise.

Beneath the moon made out of cheese,
Where penguins sip their lemon tea,
The marbles plot a grand escape,
Reaching for the bumblebee.

So if you find a rainbow cat,
Just nod and go about your way,
For every thought can spiral free,
In the land where nonsense plays.

Sunbeams Over Sultry Surrealism

A cactus wearing flip-flops struts,
Under sunbeams made of spice,
While fish with wings take evening strolls,
And turtles roll the dice.

The clouds, they laugh like tickled kids,
As jellyfish bounce on trampoline,
The breeze is warm like freshly baked,
While lemons burst in shades of green.

Marshmallow trees sway to the beat,
Of candy-coated symphonies,
Pineapple suns that dance and sing,
A feast of sweet fantasies.

So grab a hopscotch made of dreams,
And skip right into that bright ray,
For everything is quite absurd,
In this funny, sunny play.

The Curious Cupcake Conspiracy

In a bakery where muffins scheme,
The cupcakes wear their frosting crowns,
They whisper sweet and silly dreams,
As brownies plot to take the towns.

A donut's glare, a scone's laugh loud,
As pies converge to plot their fate,
In messy bowls of custard clouds,
While ginger snaps pretend to hate.

The sprinkles form a rebel pack,
As icing swirls in restless glee,
Unite to bake a wonderland,
Where cookies roam wild and free.

So if you catch a whiff of fun,
Just know it's cake that leads the way,
For in this kitchen of delight,
Silliness is here to stay.

Rambles through the Relentless Rain

Umbrellas twirl like dizzy tops,
In puddles filled with giggles,
While rubber ducks sail paper boats,
And raindrops dance in wiggly wiggles.

A rainbow's leash is held by frogs,
As toads recite their favorite song,
While thunder finds a laughing bid,
And clouds parade the all-day long.

Slippery paths twist in delight,
As raindrops roll like tiny peas,
The world turns green, then pink, then brown,
With every splash that sets us free.

So grab your coat and one good joke,
Let laughter lead you through the rain,
For splashes tell a silly tale,
In the laughter of the mundane.

A Kaleidoscope of Keystrokes

In a digital dream, a pixel parade,
Unicorns tap-dance on keys, unafraid.
Cats write sonnets, the typos abound,
A jellybean chorus in cyberspace found.

Penguins in bowties are coding with flair,
Their floppy feet dance in rhythmic despair.
Chasing the wifi, they flap and they glide,
On a rainbow of bandwidth, they'll take you for a ride.

A toaster flips poems, quite unlike my bread,
While squirrels in suits plot the words in my head.
With coffee and chaos, they orchestrate cheer,
In a world made of giggles, where logic's unclear.

So join this mad caper, let laughter abound,
Where nonsense is king, and purples wear crowns.
Each keystroke a riddle, a puzzle to tease,
In this kaleidoscope dance, let your mind feel at ease.

The Rapture of the Ridiculous

A walrus in spectacles recites a grand play,
While ducks in their tuxes just waddle away.
Marshmallows giggle from fat fluffy clouds,
As owls tell secrets to unruly crowds.

The moon wears pajamas, it's quite the sight,
With fireflies buzzing a symphony bright.
Kites made of candy soar high in the blue,
Painting the sky with a sugary hue.

Hippos in spacesuits float high and they croon,
While llamas juggle planets with whimsical tunes.
Teapots chime softly, each gadget goes wild,
In this rapture of whimsy, we dance like a child.

So gather your giggles, let's stir up a cheer,
As nonsense erupts, bringing joy far and near.
The world made of laughter, a riddle we chase,
In the rapture of ridiculous, let's frolic with grace.

Whispers of the Unseen

In the corner, a sock giggles,
Pants that prance and wiggle.
Cupcakes rain from the ceiling,
Silly folks know this feeling.

Cats wear hats made of cheese,
Shouting secrets with the breeze.
Silliness floats on the air,
Laughter's magic everywhere.

Pillow fights with purple puff,
Chasing dreams, it's just enough.
Spoon and fork doing a jig,
Dancing round, they're quite the dig.

Pickles play the tambourine,
Sing a song that's never seen.
All the nonsense comes alive,
In a world where we all thrive.

Shadows Dancing on the Ceiling

A shadow winks with a grin,
Stirring up the fun within.
Chairs are tap dancing their way,
While the lamps join in the play.

Curtains wave like they're in on it,
Twirling, swaying, not to quit.
Whispers of what's out of sight,
Tickling toes in the night.

Toasters toast in rhythmic beat,
While comics in the fridge compete.
All of this behind our eyes,
Where the twisted laughter lies.

Butterflies in tutus prance,
Inviting us to join their dance.
Through the quirky, joyous spree,
Every shadow sets us free.

Dreams Entwined in Fog

Fog rolls in on a skateboard,
Dreams not lost but simply stored.
Socks balloon at every turn,
In the mist, the giggles burn.

Pickles swim in nacho lakes,
Flying pigs on silly brakes.
Clouds are fluffing up the day,
As the moon brings out its play.

Balloons chatter like old friends,
While the laughter never ends.
In this whirl of dreamy sights,
Anything, or not, ignites.

Bicycles without a wheel,
Float along, it's quite the deal.
Foggy whispers loud and clear,
In this nonsense, we hold dear.

The Color of Confusion

A rainbow sings a silly song,
Colors clash where they belong.
Purple ducks swim in orange pools,
While jellybeans dance with fools.

Twirling around in polka dots,
Touching skies with candy thoughts.
Confusion wears a goofy hat,
Poking fun at where we're at.

Sneakers cartwheel down the street,
Chasing sunshine, oh so sweet.
Every brushstroke laughs aloud,
Painting smiles within the crowd.

In this world of silly dreams,
Everything is cut at seams.
The color spreads; it can't be tamed,
In our minds, it's always framed.

Lullabies of Lost Logic

In a land where cats wear hats,
And turtles dance on roller skates,
With whispers of pancakes singing tunes,
    Beneath the moon that levitates.

Fish swim in teacups, sipping air,
While elephants play hopscotch on clouds,
They giggle at rabbits selling rare,
    Balloons shaped like laughing cows.

A clock strikes thirteen, it's lunchtime soon,
    As stars play chess with candy bars,
    Chasing rainbows in neon spoons,
        In a world that's far from ours.

So close your eyes, let dreams take flight,
    On unicorns that ride the breeze,
    For logic's lost, and that's alright—
        In this whimsical, weird breeze.

Meandering Through Mysterious Meanings

The sun wears sunglasses, sipping tea,
While shadows play cards with the breeze,
A fish gives a speech in a tree,
Saying, 'Frogs do a waltz with ease.'

Clouds gossip softly, wearing grins,
About kittens who paint with their paws,
And the purple thoughts of sneaky twins,
That talk to beetles without a cause.

Muffins proclaim they're the best at hide,
Each crumb is a clue to find the prize,
While pickles wear hats that tilt to the side,
And donuts debate with twinkling eyes.

Let's dance with the giggles of nonsense bright,
Where logic's just a silly game,
We'll twirl and spin till the morning light,
In a song without a name.

The Joy of Jumbled Journeys

Bicycles fly on lollipop streams,
While pancakes drop beats for a dance,
Each step is sweet, filled with silly dreams,
As tractors take off in a prancing trance.

With socks as our maps, we wander wide,
Where marriages bloom between socks and shoes,
On sidewalks of candy, we take the ride,
Trading gummy worms for the latest news.

The grass hums mumbling tunes of delight,
As we chase after daisies who laugh,
In a jam where the stars twinkle bright,
And floorboards faultlessly take a photograph.

So let's tiptoe down this ticklish way,
With giggles and grins as our guide,
Through paths where the chuckles freely play,
In this rambunctious joyride.

Petals of Peculiar Perception

Flowers debate the taste of the sun,
While shadows play hide-and-seek with the light,
In gardens where playful ideas run,
Kites dip and dive, what a refreshing sight!

Daisies in tuxedos, ready to spin,
While sunbeams toast marshmallows on toast,
And winds weave jokes in a merry din,
As realities tease and gently boast.

A hedgehog conducts the symphony loud,
With trumpets made of celery stalks,
As mangoes dance for the gossiping crowd,
In this bazaar where laughter talks.

So let laughter be our guiding thread,
Through floral realms of whimsy bright,
Where nonsense blooms and logic has fled,
In petals of perception, we take flight.

The Eccentricity of Celestial Cats

In space, where no feline would dare,
They dance on the moons without a care.
Whiskers twitching to cosmic beats,
Chasing stardust and cosmic treats.

Their tails twirl like comets in flight,
Purring softly in the deep, dark night.
Galaxies twinkle in wide-eyed glee,
As they sip from the Milky Way's tea.

With hats made of stars and shoes of light,
They tumble through clouds, oh what a sight!
Napping on rings of Saturn's embrace,
These cosmic cats put us all in our place.

So if you spy a cat on a star,
Join the dance, it's never too far.
For in this realm of bizarre delight,
Cat dreams are woven in stardust bright.

Sighs Between Stars

A sigh floats softly on a galactic breeze,
Echoing whispers from cosmic trees.
They share their secrets to the night sky,
While comets wink and wearing bows tie.

Stars hang low, like lanterns aglow,
Each sigh a giggle, a bubbly show.
They chatter in glimmers, a sparkly spree,
While the Milky Way spills its creamy tea.

Between each twinkling, a joke unfolds,
The kind that even the cosmos holds.
With a wink and a nudge, stars start to laugh,
This universe is a quirky giraffe.

So listen close to the sighs up high,
For they tell the tales that never die.
In the silence of space, where laughter gleams,
We soar through the night on whimsical dreams.

A Parade of Peculiar People

In a town made of jelly and cotton candy,
Walk jumbled folks, all sorts and handy.
With bright purple hats and shoes shaped like fish,
Each step a jig, fulfilling a wish.

A man with a trumpet that sprays out confetti,
Plays tunes that dance like a fish on spaghetti.
While ladies in bloomers, defying the laws,
Twirl in circles, waving their paws.

Children on stilts made of shimmering dreams,
Skip through puddles of fizzy moonbeams.
They juggle their laughter, all the world's quirks,
As the merriment hums, igniting their smirks.

So join the parade, with a skip and a shimmy,
Through the streets so sticky and whimsically slimy.
In a land where oddity reigns like a king,
Let your heart flutter, and your spirit take wing.

The Fantasy of Forsaken Words

Lost in a book with pages that grin,
Words play hide and seek, beneath my skin.
They twirl like dancers in a grand ballet,
Hoping to find their place in the fray.

Whispers of nonsense float through the air,
Spinning tales of dragons with fur and a glare.
Syllables chuckle, as vowels take flight,
Consonants giggle in beams of soft light.

Defying the meanings, they tumble and roll,
Together they rally, a whimsical stroll.
With each little quirk, they break every rule,
In this land of nonsense, they're nobody's fool.

So gather these words and let them run wild,
In a world full of giggles, forever a child.
In the chaos of letters, fun finds its way,
A fantasy blooms where nonsense holds sway.

Laughter in a Labyrinth

In a maze of giggles and grins,
Where tickles are as standard as wins,
Jesters dance on fluffy clouds,
Making mischief beneath bright shrouds.

Socks paired wrong, a twist of fate,
Jellybeans on ducks that skate,
Echoing laughter down the halls,
While pizza dreams tumble and fall.

Chasing shadows of whispers dear,
Silly hats that appear and adhere,
Caught in a whirlwind of playful sound,
In this delightful place, joy is found.

So come, let's wander far and wide,
Through this quirky, giggly ride,
Where nonsense reigns both day and night,
And laughter keeps the heart alight.

Doodles of a Daydreamer

A pencil spins in swirling grace,
Sketching worlds that time can't trace,
Fish in hats and trees that sing,
Where candy rains and giggles spring.

Cloudy minds with colors bright,
Painting nonsense, pure delight,
A bouncing ball with polka dots,
In a sea of thought, confusion plots.

scribbled highs and doodled lows,
Chasing trains that don't quite go,
Winking stars that twirl and glide,
In this dreamscape, we confide.

So dip your brush in laughter's hue,
And let your wildest visions brew,
For every doodle tells a tale,
In a world where whimsy will prevail.

Fragments of a Forgotten Thought

Scattered bits of laughter's core,
Memories that roll on the floor,
A cookie crumb and a bouncing shoe,
Tales of nonsense, a whimsical view.

Pondering oddities, yonder sights,
Like dancing spoons and flying kites,
Echoes of chuckles float in the air,
As silly riddles with no answer stare.

Toast that sings and clocks that speak,
A rainbow jumps, a jellybean sneak,
Serendipity holds the door ajar,
With whimsical wonders, we travel far.

So gather these fragments, take them home,
In this realm where daydreams roam,
For laughter's power is quite profound,
In the silly silence, joy is found.

The Echoes of Silly Silence

In quiet corners, laughter sneaks,
Finding joy in what it speaks,
Whispers soft like cotton candy,
Mischievous tones that feel quite dandy.

The hush holds secrets, humor's light,
As giggles play at a game of fright,
Invisible pranks and winks exchanged,
In this stillness where giggles are arranged.

A silent shout, a chuckle's breeze,
Floating high among the trees,
Echoes of nonsense, softly blend,
Creating a haven where laughter won't end.

So listen close in silent nights,
For silly echoes give delights,
In the stillness, absurdity lies,
Where joy and laughter never die.

The Language of Lost Echoes

Whispers flit on gossamer wings,
Chasing shadows that laughter brings.
A yawn from a cat, a chuckle from trees,
Every sound dances, a mind's tease.

Echoes flip like pancakes on a grill,
Tickling the air, they're bound to thrill.
Cucumbers shout, and then they smirk,
As silly as a rainbow taking a quirk.

Gumdrops gossip about the sky,
While twinkling stars wink and fly.
The giggle of frogs, the sigh of the night,
In a jumbled world, everything is light.

So tread lightly on this realms of dreams,
Where nonsense is sweet, or so it seems.
A chorus of chuckles, a melody bright,
In the language of echoes, we find delight.

Dancing with Dandelion Wishes

Dandelions twirl in the afternoon glow,
Spinning tales where the wild wind blows.
Their seeds take flight, each a tiny dream,
Whispering secrets as soft as cream.

A frog in a top hat starts to tap dance,
Inviting the bees to join in the prance.
With every hop, a giggle flows,
As daisies keep count in mismatched rows.

Lollipops march to a candy parade,
While licorice snakes in the sunlight braid.
The clouds wear socks, oh what a sight,
As umbrellas laugh and spin with delight.

So let's waltz with wishes across the green,
In fields of delight where no one's ever mean.
With dandelions swirling, we'll laugh and sway,
In this whimsical world, come join the play!

Comets in a Teacup

A comet brews in a porcelain mug,
Sipping stardust, feeling snug.
Laughter bubbles in every swirl,
While marshmallow moons begin to twirl.

Teaspoons dance on the rim of dreams,
Creating laughter in sweet little streams.
With every sip, the universe winks,
As reality playfully bathes and shrinks.

Sugar cubes pirouette in delight,
While tea leaves whisper secrets of night.
The tablecloth giggles, what a fair sight,
As clowns serve cupcakes with sprinkles so bright.

In this teacup, where comets collide,
We're sipping the cosmos, with joy as our guide.
So join in the fun with a sip and a grin,
In a galaxy brewed with the laughter within!

Chasing Phantoms Through the Mist

Phantoms flutter like whispers of dew,
Chasing the moon in a game meant for two.
With capes made of bubbles, they swirl and fly,
Tickling the branches as they pass by.

A jolly old ghost plays hide and seek,
In a foggy embrace, it's a game quite unique.
With lanterns aglow, they dance in the night,
Chasing the giggles till morning's soft light.

Marshmallow clouds float in giddy delight,
As shadows and stardust twirl in their flight.
The laughter of phantoms calls from afar,
While specks of pure joy congregate like a star.

So let's follow the laughter in the cool swirling haze,
Where phantoms and dreams weave whimsical ways.
The mist is a canvas where giggles paint bright,
Chasing the echoes till the morning light.

The Dance of Disconnected Dreams

In the land where socks wear hats,
And the cats play chess with bats,
The moon sings songs of silly glee,
While jellybeans dance with giddy tea.

A rainbow strolls on polka-dotted lanes,
Twirling umbrellas in the light of trains,
Worms in top hats waddle by the stream,
As giggles echo in a wobbling dream.

Flying fishes wear funky shoes,
Tangoing with the lavender blues,
Marshmallow clouds float in the breeze,
Tickling the twinkling stars with ease.

So let your thoughts all take a spin,
Shake off the logic, let the fun begin,
In this dance of dreams, we're free to glide,
On a rainbow slide, where laughter won't hide.

Curious Curlicues in the Cosmos

In the corners of space where the whispers twirl,
A teapot's lid lifts, and a comet's a pearl,
The stars giggle brightly in spirals and swirls,
As cupcakes orbit in pastel unfurls.

The sun wears sunglasses, a comical sight,
Playing hopscotch with shadows at night,
Planets twist and twirl with a jumpy refrain,
While space squirrels chase after popcorn with gain.

Galaxies dance to the tune of a tune,
Waltzing together under the glaring moon,
With candy-cones sprouting on each asteroid,
A whimsical world that cannot be spoiled.

So lift up your gaze to this circus so grand,
Join the get-together, take a stand,
In curious curlicues, smiles abound,
In laughter and joy, our hearts will be found.

Hazy Visions of a Whirlwind Mind

In the whirlpool's heart where the puddles collide,
A juggling hedgehog takes a wild ride,
Socks have debates with invisible friends,
While wobbly turtles plot all the trends.

The bubbles burst with a pop and a fizz,
Tickling the senses with what-was-that-whiz,
Doughnuts rain down on the upside-down floor,
And nonsense delivers knock-knock at the door.

A cloud of confetti drifts lazily by,
With rubber ducks launching towards the sky,
Lollipops whisper secrets to bees,
As thoughts swirl around in the oddities' breeze.

So come take a stroll where nonsense leads,
In this labyrinth of laughter, the heart supersedes,
In hazy visions, let smiles unwind,
With every tickle of a whirlwind mind.

The Sound of a Colorful Confusion

In the symphony of jelly and jam,
Seashells gossip about a shy clam,
With a trumpet that plays just out of tune,
As balloons debate the shape of the moon.

A parrot recites poetry in rhymes,
While squirrels tap-dance and chew on limes,
The grass sings songs of an acorn's quest,
In this noisy world, humor's the best.

The stickers giggle while dancing in rows,
With colors so bright, it tickles the nose,
A cupcake breeze floats on cotton candy air,
In this colorful chaos, there's love everywhere.

So crank up the laughter, give chaos a cheer,
In this theater of nonsense, let go of your fear,
For in the sound of confusion, we find our song,
Where laughter and whimsy forever belong.

Whirls of Whimsical Wandering

In a world where jellybeans float,
And turtles wear tiny coats,
Come dance with a cat in a hat,
While sipping on fizzy moonlight.

Roundabout roads made of cheese,
With whispers of giddy bumblebees,
We'll skip through the clouds on a kite,
And laugh till the stars wave goodnight.

Socks on the ceiling, a hat on the floor,
We twirl with the spoons, then we giggle some more,
As puddles of gumdrops spill from the sky,
With tickles and giggles, we'll surely fly.

So come take a trip through this wacky scene,
Where nonsense reigns, and life's a routine,
With each goofy step, let your spirit ignite,
In the whirls of this wander, everything's light.

A Chaotic Canvas of Colors

Splashing violet across the green,
A fish in a top hat, quite the scene,
With polka dot clouds marching in rows,
And crayon trees where the laughter glows.

Twirl of orange, a wink of blue,
Unicorns dance in a vibrant queue,
A rainbow spills laughter on the ground,
With each brushstroke, silliness is found.

Swirls of glitter tickle our feet,
While paintbrushes jiggle to a nonsensical beat,
We'll sketch silly faces on ripened pears,
And giggle at puddles of bubblegum stares.

So let's paint the skies with glee today,
In this chaotic world, we'll frolic and play,
With colors that tumble and blend every hue,
In a canvas of joy, there's always room for two.

Serenade of Silly Specters

In the moonlight, they giggle and dance,
With socks on their heads, they take a chance,
Silly specters twirl in a bright moonbeam,
Whispering secrets, an outrageous dream.

They glide on the breeze with hats made of cheese,
As laughter surrounds them, a tickling tease,
With candy cane wands and marshmallow shoes,
They sing to the stars while hiding their snooze.

A lollipop moon beams down with a grin,
While jello-shaped clouds are where they begin,
Each shadow a partner in whimsical fun,
A serenade of spirits, all on the run.

So let's join the specters, oh what a sight,
In this echo of laughter, from day into night,
With giggles and glee, we'll play till it's dawn,
In this silly serenade, let the fun carry on.

The Fable of the Fluffy Unicorn

Once there lived a unicorn, fluffy and bright,
With glittering hooves that danced in the light,
He pranced through the meadows with great delight,
Spreading joy and silliness, oh what a sight!

His mane was a rainbow, so glorious and bold,
With tales of adventure waiting to be told,
Each flutter he made, magical stories spun,
In gardens of laughter, together we run.

The fluffy unicorn, he twinkled and played,
With bubbles of giggles and games that he made,
He taught all the critters, from rabbits to deer,
That life's a big joke, so let's give a cheer!

So in this fable, remember the fun,
Be silly and bright, like the unicorn run,
For laughter's the magic that we all embrace,
And fluffy adventures bring smiles to our face.

The Dreamweaver's Delight

In a land where socks all sing,
Trees wear hats and birds take wing.
The moon's a pie, the sun's a scoop,
With giggles swirling in a loop.

Invisible cats dance on air,
While jelly beans hang without a care.
Chasing shadows, we leap and twirl,
In this whimsical, wobbly whirl.

Each dream floats by on candy clouds,
Laughing quietly, it draws in crowds.
We sail on waves of purple glee,
With silly grins, we run carefree.

So gather round, take off your shoes,
In this delight, we'll never lose.
The Dreamweaver smiles, with a wink,
In a realm where giggles always sync.

The Topsy-Turvy Tale

Once, a fish rode a bicycle fast,
While cows in tuxedos danced and laughed.
Umbrellas rained down sprinkles of fun,
A topsy-turvy world had begun.

Boxes walked, and shoes could talk,
Trees drummed softly on the block.
With flapping hats and bouncing shoes,
Everyone joined in the joyful hues.

Yet, wise old snails played chess at noon,
Underneath a giant disco moon.
Pigs flew high, on candyfloss kites,
In this tale of pure, silly delights.

So flip a joke and spin a yarn,
In lands where chaos creates charm.
With laughter drumming on our hearts,
In a topsy-turvy tale, fun starts.

Carnival of the Curious Clouds

Welcome to the carnival high,
Where giggles float up to the sky.
Clowns with bicycles made of cheese,
Perform tricks that bring us to our knees.

Cotton candy elephants parade by,
While popcorn rain falls from the sky.
In this fair, there's always a surprise,
As we watch with wide, curious eyes.

Fluffy bunnies juggle moonbeams bright,
While stars play hide and seek at night.
The merry-go-round spins silly tales,
On rainbow paths where fun prevails.

So grab a seat on this wild ride,
Let laughter be your joyful guide.
In this carnival, we lose the frowns,
Among the curious, spinning clouds.

The Enigmatic Essence of Ether

In a world of questions, swirling bright,
Where whispers dance, and thoughts take flight.
A pickle plays chess with a wise old hat,
While jellyfish swing with a tip of fat.

In curious realms where odd things play,
The sun winks bright at the end of day.
Muffins wear shoes, dancing with flair,
In riddles wrapped up in the air.

As clocks run backward, giggles ensue,
With thoughts so wild, yet strangely true.
In this essence, we drift and delve,
Finding joy in nonsense, ourselves.

So twist a thought, let laughter free,
In the ether, where we weave glee.
Each puzzling moment, a gift we share,
In the enigmatic magic of the air.

Whimsy on the Wind

A kite flies high, with socks for wings,
It softly hums, and sweetly sings.
The clouds wear hats, made of butter,
As rainbows dance in puddles of clutter.

The grass gets tickled by playful bristles,
While squirrels juggle with crunchy pistils.
A tree sprouted shoes, oh what a sight,
And everyone's laughing, in pure delight.

A snail in a tux, he waltzes so grand,
While ants do a conga, hand in hand.
The sun throws confetti, a vibrant show,
As whispers of giggles in the breezes blow.

In this world that flutters, where oddities roam,
Each corner a joke, each nook a poem.
So float on a paper boat, hold tight to the grin,
For whimsy awaits, let the fun begin!

The Unraveling of a Daydream

In a land where the cats wear shoes,
A pastry chef's fond of green bean stews.
Dancing teapots and bouncing chairs,
Whistling wind plays with light hearted flares.

The sun peeks in with a cheeky wink,
While fish on bicycles swim in a drink.
There's chocolate rain and candy trees,
With gummy bears sipping herbal teas.

The clocks all giggle, tick-tock like a tune,
And spoons play tag with the light of the moon.
A frog in a cape, strikes a pose so bold,
With stories of laughter that never grow old.

Awake in this dream with amorphous delight,
Where nonsense thrives in the softest light.
Let out a chuckle, for dreams are the key,
To a world that's whimsical, wild, and free!

Moonbeams and Marbles

Under the stars, marbles roll and gleam,
Chasing the shadows, like whispers of cream.
A moonbeam giggles, and tickles the night,
While owls wear glasses, looking quite bright.

The crickets are DJs, spinning their tunes,
As fireflies flash like cheeky cartoons.
The grass grows tall, with shoes made of lace,
And friendly wind sweeps us up for a race.

Jellybeans fluff in a starry parade,
Where unicorns prance, in colors they made.
A teapot winks, as it puffs out a sigh,
While sprightly begonia is learning to fly.

So gather your marbles, let's bounce them about,
With laughter and nonsense, here's no room for doubt.
In a world of moonbeams, let giggles ignite,
For this merry chaos is purest delight!

The Curious Case of the Woolly Moon

The woolly moon sits snug and round,
With a knitted scarf that the stars have found.
It whispers soft tales to the clouds above,
As nightingales croon songs of silly love.

Each cranny and nook is filled with surprise,
As the moon places buttons on sleepy eyes.
With sheep dancing round in a fluffy ballet,
Saying goodbye to the silliness of day.

A cat in pajamas plays hide and seek,
While pancakes flip in a syrupy peak.
And owls wear mustaches, oh isn't it sweet?
As giggles and chuckles make nighttime complete.

So catch the moon's laughter, woven in dreams,
A tale of the wacky, where whimsy redeems.
In this curious case, let your joys shine bright,
With a wink from the moon, and a heart full of light!

Enigmatic Echoes of Everyday Life

Where teapots dance and socks do sing,
Giggling at the little things.
Bananas wear hats, so spry and bright,
While toasters toast under moonlight.

Cacti in tutus sway with grace,
As jellybeans race in a racy chase.
The clouds are made of fluffy cheese,
Whispering secrets with each breeze.

Umbrellas parade in the sunny delight,
While fish ride bikes with great insight.
Silly shadows leap without a care,
In this absurd scene where all things share.

With every turn, the odd takes flight,
Lifting our spirits, hearts feel light.
With giggles and chuckles, we'll embrace the fun,
In this wacky world, we all are one.

Whirls of Whimsy in a Wistful Wind

The wind is a painter with colors bright,
Spinning tales under moonlit night.
Twirling umbrellas chase curious cats,
While sunsets wear polka-dotted hats.

A jingle of keys sings a silly tune,
As crickets dance to the light of the moon.
Butterflies giggle, fluttering 'round,
Finding joy in the silliest sound.

The trees play peek-a-boo with the sun,
As squirrels in tuxedos start to run.
A conga line of ants in a daze,
Celebrate life in quirky ways.

Whirls of laughter swirl in the air,
Tickling the toes of those unaware.
In this merry breeze, let worries rescind,
Join the parade of the whimsy wind.

The Jester's Jigsaw Puzzle

In a box made of laughter, pieces lie,
Reluctant sprinkles of cheese up high.
Cats wear shoes that are three sizes too big,
While jigsaw pieces dance a wild jig.

The king of crayons rules the land,
Mixing colors with a bubblegum hand.
Rubber ducks leap on a water slide,
In a party where happiness won't hide.

Each piece a giggle, each fit a cheer,
As the puzzle forms over cups of cheer.
Giggles and wiggles come together here,
In the kingdom of nonsense, all hold dear.

Countdown the seconds with a silly face,
As the jester's laughter fills the space.
Join the madcap fun in this quirky hustle,
Together we solve the jester's puzzle.

A Mirthful Maze of Whispers

Within a maze of candy twists,
Chocolate rabbits lead with gentle winks.
Marshmallow clouds float up above,
While gummy bears radiate grins of love.

Whispers of giggles weave through the space,
As comical critters dance in place.
Each corner reveals a surprise so sweet,
With lollipop trees and licorice feet.

The whirl of whimsy guides every turn,
Chasing the laughter, letting it burn.
Spinning in circles, let out a cheer,
For joy is the treasure we all hold dear.

Through the mirthful maze, we'll find our way,
With every chuckle brightening the day.
In this land of delight, let worries be far,
As we roam through these shades of bizarre.

The Laughing Lighthouse Keeper

The keeper chuckled at the waves,
As they danced like silly braves.
His light giggled through the night,
Guiding ships with comical light.

Seagulls wore hats made of lace,
Flapping wildly in the race.
Each horn blast laughed, full of cheer,
To greet the fog that wandered near.

On stormy nights, he'd tell a tale,
Of jellyfish that tried to sail.
With voices high and squeaky glee,
They'd sip on fog like lemonade tea.

Oh, how the stars would crack a grin,
As lighthouse beams spun tales within.
A cosmic party, laughter spread,
The keeper grinned, then went to bed.

Spinning Stories from Cloud Dust

A rabbit danced atop a cloud,
Twirling tales, he laughed out loud.
With cotton candy in his hand,
He spun great stories across the land.

The raindrops joined a conga line,
While sunbeams giggled, feeling fine.
Each flash of light was pure delight,
In this wacky, whimsical night.

The moon threw a party, bright and grand,
Inviting clouds to join the band.
Each plucky puff would crack a joke,
As stars blinked back with merry smoke.

With every tale, the world would sway,
In fluffy dreams where nonsense played.
So let's all join that cloud parade,
For laughter lives where dreams are made.

The Curious Chronicles of Colorful Creatures

In fields where purple frogs wear crowns,
And turtles sport the brightest gowns,
A party brews with colors bright,
As creatures twirl in pure delight.

The flamingos burst into a song,
While dandelions danced along.
Each whisper swept through grassy lanes,
In silly tales where giggles reign.

A parrot juggled apples, bold,
And told great tales of mischief told.
With colors swirling in a show,
They painted rainbows on the toe.

So gather round, you creatures weird,
Spread laughter wide and never feared.
In this odd world, let joy not cease,
For nonsense reigns and never leaves.

Murmurs Among the Mercurial Moonbeams

The moonbeams chuckle, light as air,
Spreading giggles everywhere.
They murmur softly, tales they weave,
Of dancing shadows that deceive.

A comet zooms, a sparkly sprite,
Tickling stars with sheer delight.
Each twinkle winks with gleeful glee,
As twilight holds its secrets free.

Down below, the critters grin,
As moonbeams dance, they join in.
With shadows stretching far and wide,
They leap and spin, no need to hide.

So let the night be filled with cheer,
As whispers of the beams draw near.
In this frolicsome, cosmic play,
Laughter blooms in a bright ballet.

Scribbles from the Silly Side

In a garden of giggles, ducks wear hats,
Bouncing upside down, where the cat chitchats.
Pigs on pogo sticks leap to the skies,
While goldfish recite the world's best lies.

Jellybeans dance on the ceiling high,
Kites that speak French twist and fly.
The cow plays chess with a dancing flea,
As pancakes race in the grand jamboree.

Bubblegum trees drip sticky pink dew,
While a frog in sunglasses croons a tune.
Toasters play hopscotch, with bread on their heads,
A circus of nonsense, where logic now dreads.

Join the parade of the whimsically weird,
Where giggles are eaten, and frowns are all smeared.
In this carnival of quirk, let your heart glide,
Through scribbles of joy from the silly side.

Bursts of Bewildering Bliss

A snail wore a cape, and flew through the air,
With jellyfish friends playing musical chairs.
Rainclouds threw parties, splashing with cheer,
As cupcakes flew by with a sprinkle of beer.

The sun wore swirls like a peppermint twist,
While clouds played charades in a fluffy mist.
A parade of confetti tornadoed the street,
Where hedgehogs on scooters tried out fancy feet.

Sardines sang opera, while pickles would dance,
And crumpets recited their strange little stance.
With giggles as fuel and joy as the aim,
In this burst of bliss, let nothing feel tame.

So revel in realms of absurdity grand,
Where laughter ignites like a warm, friendly hand.
In a world so bizarre, let your heart sway,
In bursts of bewildering bliss, come and play!

The Spiraling Saga of Sleeping Squirrels

Squirrels in slippers are snoozing away,
Nestled in nut-boxes, they dream and they play.
Uncle acorn narrates tales of delight,
While pinecones, the audience, giggle at night.

In the spiral of dreams, they soar through the trees,
With chocolate-chip clouds, dancing in the breeze.
Each nutty adventure, so silly and bright,
Unravels in laughter, a whimsical flight.

One twirls with a leaf, another rides a snail,
While their sleepy escapades turn into a tale.
From moss-covered couches, to gumdrop galas,
These whimsical dreams are pure airborne balas.

So as they slumber, with joy and with cheer,
The saga unfolds in the hush of the year.
In the spiraling saga, may we all find repose,
Among sleeping squirrels, a life that just glows.

Shadows of Haphazard Happenings

Shadows play hopscotch on polka-dotted ground,
As teapots hold tennis matches, quite profound.
A lobster in pajamas reads books in the park,
While squirrels perform magic, sparking a lark.

Flamingos juggle donuts with elegant flair,
And monkeys recite poems in midair!
The moon sprinkles laughter on night-time's embrace,
As rainbows conspire to join in the race.

With socks on their ears, and hats made of cheese,
The penguins align for a wild game of freeze.
Each haphazard moment creates such a show,
In the shadows of nonsense, all giggles will grow.

Join hands with the quirky, let silliness reign,
Embrace every shadow with laughter unchained.
In this wacky world where chaos takes flight,
Dance in the shadows, and bask in the light!

The Absurdity of Floating Giraffes

Giraffes in the sky, oh what a sight,
With polka dots dancing, they flutter in flight.
They sip on the stars and munch on the clouds,
While laughing at pigeons and playful crowds.

A top hat they wear, tipped just from grace,
They twirl and they spin in an endless race.
With necks far too long for the ground down below,
They giggle at cats who say, "Where'd they go?"

Threads of a Twisted Yarn

In a closet of colors, where socks disappear,
Yarns weave tales of absurdity clear.
A cat made of buttons plays tag with a shoe,
While spoons sing a duet with a dancing goose.

Crocheted clouds rain jellybeans bright,
As laughter erupts from a fluffy delight.
The fabric of nonsense, so tangled and fun,
Cuddles you close till the day is done.

Riddles Wrapped in Time

A clock talks in riddles, tick-tock, tick-say,
While spoons solve puzzles that withered away.
The sun wears a scarf of spaghetti and cheese,
And tickles the moon just to tease the breeze.

Time travels in bubbles, all squiggly and bright,
As history giggles at morning's delight.
Questions float freely like butterflies bold,
While answers show up in a language of gold.

Fragments of a Broken Kaleidoscope

A shattered kaleidoscope, colors in flight,
Spins tales of penguins wearing hats oh so tight.
They tango with turtles on roller skates fast,
While rainbows applaud with a thunderous blast.

Each fragment a puzzle, each piece a dream,
Silly scenarios unravel and beam.
In this world of nonsense, where giggles collide,
Laughter is the compass, let it be your guide.

Oddities in Everyday Parades

A penguin dances with a spoon,
Wearing a hat that looks like a moon.
Cats throw confetti, dogs bark in glee,
As rubber ducks float down the marquee.

There's a man on stilts made of pie,
With jellybean shoes that can surely fly.
The marching band plays tunes from the sea,
While a goat leads the way on a bright green tree.

High in the sky, a piglet drew,
A map of snacks on a giant moo.
Balloons shaped like fish kiss squirrels on bikes,
As twirling giraffes juggle sparkly spikes.

At the end of the path, all gather and cheer,
For carnival cakes that taste just like beer.
The day ends with laughs, oh, what a charade,
In a world where oddities often invade.

A Medley of Muddle and Mischief

There's a cupcake thief with a hat made of cheese,
Who tap dances lightly on the bumblebee breeze.
A llama in pajamas steals flowers for fun,
While juggling with jelly in the bright summer sun.

The clock strikes thirteen, then goes back to two,
As the fish in the pond start reciting a clue.
A turtle in sneakers chases after a kite,
Drawing rainbows in chalk, oh, what a sight!

An octopus chef pours soup from a shoe,
While squirrels perform tango, looking quite blue.
A parade of confusion, a train full of glee,
Wanders through laughter, just come and see!

With pastries that giggle atop the town square,
And squirrels making selfies with a swing in the air.
The day ends with chaos, all winks and nods,
In a realm of delight, where nonsense applauds.

The Enigma of Lopsided Lighthouses

There's a lighthouse that leans, just a tad too much,
Painting the sky in hues that you can't touch.
With light that goes left while the waves go right,
It's known for its giggles, not guiding by night.

A seagull in stripes shrieks riddles of woe,
While jellyfish bounce in a jelly-like show.
They dance on the rocks as the sun starts to fade,
And sing of the tales that the barnacles made.

Why does a boat wear a tutu and sing?
It's all for the fish—what joy they bring!
As sandcastles whisper the secrets of sea,
To the moonlight that twinkles both wild and free.

So let's gather 'round for a most curious sight,
With lopsided lighthouses lighting the night.
In a world where the odd and the joyful collide,
Every moment's a puzzle we can't help but ride.

Fantasies Lost in a Fog

A fog rolled in wearing pajamas and socks,
Hiding the turtles while peek-a-boo knocks.
A dragon with hiccups breathes bubbles of tea,
While gnomes ride the vapors, all frolicking free.

The sun plays hide and seek with a cloud,
While whispers of jellybeans gather a crowd.
A hedgehog in glasses claims wisdom and lore,
While dancing on rainbows that twinkle and soar.

Balloons float by, each one tells a tale,
Of marshmallow mountains and candy cane trails.
As shadows giggle, the moon spins around,
In the fog of confusion, joy long is found.

So come take a stroll in this whimsical mist,
Where nothing makes sense and dear nonsense persists.
In a land full of laughter, where dreams all belong,
Every fog-draped moment bursts into song.

Twists and Turns of a Topsy-Turvy World

In a world where fish can fly,
And the sun greets the moon with a sigh,
Upside down trees sway and dance,
While silly clouds prance in a trance.

Pigs play poker on a rooftop high,
Beneath flamingos that paint the sky,
Lollipops sprout from the greenest grass,
And time tiptoes by, oh how it will pass!

Kites dive down for a quick parade,
As laughter bounces from shade to shade,
Jellybeans grow on the wildest vines,
Where quizzical squirrels weave silly lines.

So twirl with me in this fractured place,
Where nonsense is a dance, a cheerful grace,
With topsy-turvy thinking so grand,
We'll write the rules with a giggling hand.

Paradoxes in a Puddle

A puddle reflects the sky so bright,
Yet when you jump in, it's a wobbly sight,
Fish with umbrellas float on by,
While ducks wear hats and curtsy shy.

Mirrors laugh as you splash around,
Giggling at feet that barely found,
Dandelions whisper absurdity sweet,
As you tango with frogs on the neat, wet street.

Rainbows fall in droplets small,
Painting puddles, a vibrant sprawl,
Each splash a burst of laughing sound,
In this paradox, joy is found.

So take off your shoes, jump in with glee,
Twirl 'round the chaos, wild and free,
For life in the puddle is bright and bold,
In this paradox of nonsense, behold!

Whimsical Wonders of a Wandering Mind

Through a garden where thoughts grow strange,
Marshmallow flowers rearrange,
Butterflies muse with polka-dot wings,
As hummingbirds recite silly things.

A river flows with chocolate delight,
Where daydreams swim and take flight,
Whispers of candy dance on the breeze,
And giggles erupt from the swaying trees.

In this realm of whimsical dance,
Lemonade ponds inspire a trance,
Clouds made of cotton candy fluff,
Tickle the senses, never enough!

So wander with me through this delightful maze,
Where nonsense blooms in so many ways,
And in every corner, a giggle we find,
In the whimsical wonders of the wandering mind.

Frolicking Fables in Twilight

As twilight paints the sky with a giggle,
Owl and cat share a moonlit wiggle,
Silly shadows stretch and slide,
While snickers ripple at the night's tide.

Beneath the stars, antics abound,
With quirky tales spun all around,
A mouse in a tux juggles three cheese,
As whispers of laughter float through the trees.

Fireflies twinkle wearing tiny hats,
As lobsters dance with the chitchat of cats,
In a fable world of frolic and fun,
Where tales are spun until the night's done.

So join the frolic in this twilight gleam,
Where nonsense flows, like a humorous dream,
And beneath the stars, let laughter ignite,
In these frolicking fables that sparkle at night.

Tangles in the Tides of Time

Rubber ducks in winter snow,
Dancing to a clockwork show.
Banana peels on silver swings,
Jellybeans with paper wings.

Socks that giggle, coats that cheer,
Whisper secrets to the ear.
Tick-tock tunes from marzipan,
Chasing dreams in a candy van.

The Curious Chorus of Invisible Friends

Invisible hats on invisible heads,
Singing songs that twist like threads.
Candy canes made out of air,
Tickle monsters without a care.

Lollipops that jive and sway,
Whimsical creatures come out to play.
In a world where giggles bloom,
And shadows dance in every room.

Bubbles of Blurred Reality

Floating fish in jelly ponds,
Dancing with the magic wands.
Sipping tea from sandal-shaped cups,
Ticklish apples doing jumps.

Frosted cupcakes in the sun,
Whirlwinds made of loop-de-loops run.
Chasing rainbows, sticky, sweet,
In a world of whimsical feat.

Songs from the Enchanted Ether

Moonlight whispers in a jar,
Polka-dots on a flying car.
Muffins that can tell the time,
Chocolate rivers, oh so prime.

Giraffes in top hats take a bow,
Singing tunes to Nature's cow.
With every giggle, joy ignites,
Keep your heart in silly flights.

Jumbles in the Jigsaw Sky

In patches blue and cotton white,
A squirrel juggles stars at night.
The moon wears socks, quite out of place,
While fish on bicycles race without a trace.

Lollipops grow on trees of fluff,
Where marshmallow clouds say, "That's enough!"
A dog plays chess with a fuzzy rat,
And hats grow minds, imagine that!

The sun dons shades, a hipster find,
As rainbows giggle, intertwined.
A landscape churned from some odd stew,
What's real here? Not a single clue.

Each puzzle piece in swirling flight,
Hopscotch dances in sheer delight.
So join the game, let's lose our way,
In jumbles bright, we'll laugh and play.

Clouds with Unfinished Stories

Puffy tales float overhead,
Whispers of what the rabbits said.
A plot twist near a rainbow bend,
Where unicorns just chill and blend.

One cloud fights with a shimm'ring star,
While penguins argue near and far.
Snippets of drama in the breeze,
Gefilte fish play hopscotch with ease.

A squirrel's tale is left untold,
While ladybugs dance, brave and bold.
Each ink drop drips from twilight's pen,
Creating chaos time and again.

Frame by frame, the sky's a screen,
In every gap, a new routine.
Let's catch the breeze, let stories fly,
In unfinished realms, don't ask why!

The Riddle of Randomness

What's the color of a musical bee?
Is it purple, pink, or just a spree?
The answer, dear friend, is up for grabs,
Like spaghetti thrown at fishy crabs.

Kittens make rules in the world of fun,
As tacos play catch with the glowing sun.
A puzzle piece peeks round the bend,
Seeking logic where nonsense transcends.

Is a train made of jelly a dream we chase?
What about spoons that run in a race?
The riddles escape as we try to see,
In the garden of chaos, come dance with glee.

Count the stars that wear silly shoes,
And stumble on clouds that sing the blues.
In randomness, together we find,
A laugh, a giggle, a joyful mind.

Chasing Shadows in a Kaleidoscope

Shadows twist like gum on a shoe,
In colors that shimmer and break in two.
A flamingo winks from behind a tree,
While a giraffe juggles soft meringue tea.

Watch as the bubblegum shadows play,
In kaleidoscope worlds, we laugh and sway.
Each turn reveals a silly surprise,
A moonwalking turtle that spins and flies.

With every glance, the colors blend,
As jellybeans form a quirky trend.
Chasing reflections, we tiptoe light,
In a world of whimsy, all feels just right.

So let's break out and run with cheer,
In shadows of laughter, we've nothing to fear.
With kaleidoscopes and giggles in hand,
We'll roam through the silly, a bright wonderland.

Chronicles from the Cloudy Constellations

In the sky where the shoelaces twirl,
And paper airplanes dance, unfurl.
Cats wear hats made of cotton candy,
As cows on stilts prance, quite dandy.

Stars giggle in pajamas so bright,
While rainbows slide down a banana right.
Marshmallows play chess with the fog,
As teapots hum tunes, like a frog.

Lollipops wink from Pluto's reign,
Chasing dreams on a sweet candy train.
Balloons pop secrets in the night,
Whispers of jellybeans take flight.

So come take a trip to the whims of space,
Where nonsense is dressed in a funny face.
The chronicles scribbled in candy pen,
Will make you giggle again and again.

The Silliness of Surrealities.

A toaster sailed on a buttered breeze,
While dancing sock puppets rolled in threes.
Cupcakes debated the meaning of life,
Between spoon and fork, there sparked some strife.

Pickles wore capes, flying through the air,
As marshmallow roosters scrambled with flair.
Talking teacups spilled gossip so loud,
In a whirlwind of nonsense, they felt so proud.

Giraffes played hopscotch, oh what a sight,
While elephants twirled in the moon's soft light.
A cheese wheel sang songs from a jar of jam,
In a land where they all share a great big slam.

So revel in laughter, let whimsy unfurl,
In this quirky world, give nonsense a whirl.
The silliness found in a wibbly wobbly gleam,
Will tickle your heart like a fluffy cloud dream.

Whispers of the Wisp

A wisp of wind told tales of glee,
While giggling grass did a little spree.
Kites danced with crayons, drawing the sun,
In fields where all the fun had begun.

Fluffy clouds wore shoes, skipping with flair,
As donuts held hands with a whimsical bear.
Lollipops laughed at the ticklish breeze,
While jellybeans huddled beneath the trees.

Talking umbrellas twirled in delight,
Splashing puddles with colors so bright.
In this wacky dream where nonsense shines,
The whispers tickle like playful lines.

So float with the whispers, let laughter take flight,
In a land where the silly reigns day and night.
The wisp of fun that dances around,
Will lift your spirits off the ground.

Clouded Conundrums

In a dreamscape where fish wear hats,
And turtles zoom by on tiny spats,
The sun set on pillows stitched with giggles,
While seashells danced and did little jigs.

Pineapples rode unicycles with zest,
While frogs in tuxedos played dress-up best.
Marzipan castles perched on the hill,
Waving at clouds that popped at their will.

Pumpkins recited poems in rhyme,
To snickering squirrels, losing all time.
In a whirlwind of wonder where funny prevails,
Each riddle releases a trail of tales.

So step into this labyrinth of joy,
Where giggles and nonsense employ,
The clouded conundrums all intertwine,
Create laughter's path, oh how divine!

The Quirk of Quizzical Quokka

In a world where whimsies roam,
A quokka winks from its leafy dome.
It juggles berries, one by one,
And giggles at the rise of sun.

Its friends wear hats of fluffy fluff,
While dancing on the grass so tough.
A curious crew, they laugh and play,
In their own silly, crooked way.

With every bounce, a riddle unfurls,
As they twirl and sway, oh how it whirls!
They speak in rhymes, a jumbled tongue,
In this land of joy, forever young.

So join the fun, take off your shoes,
Let laughter spill, you cannot lose.
For in the realm of quokka glee,
Life's a riddle, wild and free.

Flashes of Fantastic Folly

A unicorn with polka dots,
Plays hopscotch on the parking lots.
Its horn a rainbow, sparkles bright,
In dreams of sugar, pure delight.

A penguin wears a woolly scarf,
As jellybeans make the daisies laugh.
With floppy boots and flappy wings,
It dances to the tune of kings.

The moon engages in a game,
As planets giggle at its fame.
A cosmic jester, round and wide,
In zero gravity, it takes a ride.

Through laughter's lens, the world transforms,
Each snap and crackle, delight in swarms.
A flash of folly in the night,
Ignites the stars, a dazzling light.

The Browsing Banshee's Bazaar

At twilight's edge, a market spins,
Where banshees shop for ghostly pins.
With carts of whispers, charms in tow,
They swap their stories, high and low.

A flower shop sells giggling blooms,
Bright as twinkling, teasing rooms.
While haunting melodies drift around,
In this odd bazaar, laughter's found.

A ghostly baker whips up treats,
Delightful shadows for hungry feats.
Sugar-coated sighs in each bite,
Haunts each evening with pure delight.

So come and browse the spirited show,
Where humor dances, and laughter flows.
In the banshee's realm, joy's the prize,
As shimmering mirth lights up the skies.

Upon the Hazy Horizon

Where clouds wear hats and dance in line,
A view of whimsy, pure and fine.
The sun spills jelly, gold and bright,
As laughter lifts the spirits light.

A squirrel sells dreams in tiny jars,
Winked at by shimmering sparring stars.
It crafts each tale with a nutty twist,
Inviting all to join the list.

Beneath the trees of dancing leaves,
A jester spins in spring's bright eves.
With every chuckle, the breezes play,
A world of nonsense, bright and gay.

So let your worries drift away,
Join in the fun, come what may.
For on this horizon, humor will thrive,
In the haze of laughter, we come alive.

The Unseen Adventure of the Floating Fern

A fern took flight one sunny day,
It danced with clouds, in playful sway.
It chatted with bees, then spun like a top,
But tripped on a breeze and went for a drop.

It landed with grace in a puddle of paint,
Shouting to frogs, 'I'm a magical saint!'
They croaked in reply, with a wink and a cheer,
'Join us in mischief, there's nothing to fear!'

The ferns took turns to float and to twirl,
Each leap and bound made their fronds swirl.
Around them, the daisies giggled aloud,
As the fern became king of its hilltop cloud.

So if you should wander where ferns take their flight,
You might just glimpse laughter that dances in light.
With friends up above and delight all around,
The unseen adventures shall always be found.

A Garden of Giggles and Grains

In a garden where giggles sprout from the ground,
The flowers tell secrets without making a sound.
They tickle the toes of those passing by,
And dance with the wind, like a jolly old guy.

The grains wear hats made of candy and thread,
While beetles play chess on the leaves overhead.
A sunflower swoons, with a sigh and a smile,
As butterflies flutter in a colorful style.

One day a potato decided to sing,
With a voice so absurd, it brightened the spring.
The onions cried laughter, their layers unfurled,
In this garden of nonsense, joy danced and twirled.

So come take a stroll, if you're feeling quite dreary,
In this realm of delight, where the silly is cheery.
From giggling grains to the laughter of blooms,
A garden of fun where joy always looms.

The Nonsense Navigator's Notes

The navigator scribbles without much sense,
His map is a riddle, his compass intense.
He notes down the clouds, the stars, and the tea,
While dancing with shadows, delightful and free.

He sails on a boat made of jelly and jam,
With a crew of wise crickets, each one a grand slam.
Through oceans of marshmallows, they float and they giggle,
While fog made of pudding makes them all wiggle.

At dawn they discover a gate made of fun,
It leads to a realm where the bright colors run.
With giggles as currency, they trade with delight,
And the sun bows low, as they party all night.

The navigator grins, with his notes all askew,
For nonsense adventures are treasures so true.
So hoist up the sails for the journey ahead,
With laughter and joy as the finest of threads.

Laughter in the Labyrinth

Within a maze of hedges so tall,
Echoes of laughter do twirl and sprawl.
Each turn hides a chuckle, each corner a snort,
As gnomes play hopscotch and ducks come to court.

Puns bounce through paths like bright summer bees,
Tickling each wanderer with moments of ease.
A ghost in a tutu twirls past with a grin,
While hedgehogs join hands, in a silly spin.

The walls whisper riddles that tickle the mind,
As shadows of humor dance, unconfined.
A flickering lantern sings songs bold and clear,
Inviting all travelers to chuckle and cheer.

So wander this twisty, whimsical trail,
Where laughter's the map and nonsense won't fail.
For in this great maze, with each step you take,
You'll find all the joy of the jester awake.

www.ingramcontent.com/pod-product-compliance
Lightning Source LLC
Chambersburg PA
CBHW072148200426
43209CB00051B/865